# Marine Tanks: The Hard Punch of America's Middle-Weight Fighting Force

## Jared R. Duff

NIMBLE BOOKS LLC: THE AI LAB FOR BOOK-LOVERS

~ FRED ZIMMERMAN, EDITOR ~

*Humans and AI making books richer, more diverse, and more surprising.*

## Publishing Information

(c) 2023 Nimble Books LLC
ISBN: 978-1-60888-275-5

## AI-generated Keyword Phrases

- Marine Tanks;
Combat environments;
Performance and capabilities;
High kinetic conventional fights;
Gulf War;
Invasion of Iraq 2003;
Unconventional high intensity environments;
Battle of Fallujah;
Role of tanks in low intensity environments;
Somalia humanitarian operations;
Superior offensive capability;
Survivability and firepower of Marine Tanks;
Importance in supporting the Marine Air Ground Task Force;

## Publisher's Notes

This 2011 thesis by a Marine Corp tank major foreshadows the controversial 2021 decision by Marine Corps Commandant David Berger to eliminate the tanks that had been part of the Marine Corps combined force for close to a century. The rationale was to free up the resources needed to rebuild the Marine Corps in alignment with expected requirements for a war in the Pacific. The decision sparked a controversy that will only truly be resolved by the outcome of war.

This annotated edition illustrates the capabilities of the AI Lab for Book-Lovers to add context and ease-of-use to manuscripts. It includes five types of abstracts, building from simplest to more complex: TLDR (one word), ELI5, TLDR (vanilla), Scientific Style, and Action Items; three essays to increase viewpoint diversity: Grounds for Dissent, Red Team Critique, and MAGA Perspective; and Notable Passages and Nutshell Summaries for each page.

## ANNOTATIONS

# ABSTRACTS

## TL;DR (ONE WORD)

Marine Tanks.

## EXPLAIN IT TO ME LIKE I'M FIVE YEARS OLD

This document is about tanks that are used by Marines in wars and other conflicts. It talks about how these tanks have done well in different types of fights, both big ones and smaller ones. It gives examples of battles where the tanks were successful. The document also says that tanks are important in helping the Marines do their job. It mentions that tanks are currently being used in Afghanistan, and talks about countries that might be a problem in the future. Overall, it says that Marine Tanks are very strong and

## TL;DR (VANILLA)

This document provides an overview of the performance and capabilities of Marine Tanks in various combat environments. It highlights their success in both conventional and unconventional fights, as well as their role in low intensity environments. The document emphasizes the offensive capability, survivability, and firepower of Marine Tanks, and mentions their current deployment in Afghanistan and potential threats from countries like North Korea, Russia, and China.

## SCIENTIFIC STYLE

This document provides an overview of the performance and capabilities of Marine Tanks in various combat environments. It highlights their success in both high kinetic conventional fights, such as the Gulf War and the invasion of Iraq in 2003, as well as in unconventional high intensity environments, using the Battle of Fallujah as an example. The document also discusses the role of tanks in low intensity environments, specifically in Somalia during humanitarian operations. It emphasizes the superior offensive capability, survivability, and firepower of Marine Tanks, and their importance in supporting the Marine Air Ground Task Force. Additionally, the document mentions the current deployment of tanks in Afghanistan and the potential threats posed by countries like North Korea, Russia, and China.

## ACTION ITEMS

Conduct further research on the specific capabilities and performance of Marine Tanks in different combat environments.

Analyze the effectiveness of Marine Tanks in supporting the Marine Air Ground Task Force and their role in combined arms operations.

Assess the potential threats posed by countries like North Korea, Russia, and China and evaluate the readiness of Marine Tanks to counter these threats.

Explore potential improvements or advancements in Marine Tank technology to enhance their offensive capability, survivability, and firepower.

Consider the lessons learned from previous deployments and engagements to inform future training and operational strategies for Marine Tanks.

# VISUAL ABSTRACTS

Figure 1. The mood is: **Marine Tank.**

The AI-generated prompt was: *Create a black and white illustration that captures the intense and powerful emotions evoked by Marine Tanks in combat. The drawing should convey the resilience, strength, and determination of these tanks as they successfully navigate through various combat environments. It should depict a Marine Tank in action, showcasing its superior offensive capability and firepower. The illustration should also convey a sense of urgency and readiness, symbolizing the importance of these tanks in supporting the Marine Air Ground Task Force. Additionally, the drawing should hint at the potential threats posed by countries like North Korea, Russia, and China, adding an element of tension to the overall mood. The emotions conveyed through this illustration should be a mix of excitement, anticipation, and caution, enticing readers to explore further into the document's contents on Marine Tanks.*

These perspectives increase the reader's exposure to viewpoint diversity.

**GROUNDS FOR DISSENT**

Disagreement on the effectiveness of Marine Tanks in unconventional high intensity environments: A member of the organization might have principled, substantive reasons to dissent from this report if they believe that the success of Marine Tanks in the Battle of Fallujah is overstated or not representative of their overall performance in unconventional high intensity environments. They may argue that the specific circumstances and terrain of Fallujah were favorable to tank operations, but that tanks may struggle in other similar situations due to limitations such as mobility in urban areas or vulnerability to asymmetric threats like improvised explosive devices (IEDs).

Concerns about the relevance of tanks in low intensity environments: Another reason for dissent could be a belief that the document overstates the importance of tanks in low intensity environments, such as Somalia during humanitarian operations. The dissenter may argue that tanks are not well-suited for such operations, where their firepower and offensive capability may be excessive or unnecessary. They might advocate for alternative solutions or resources that better align with the specific needs and challenges of low intensity environments.

Doubts about the future viability of tanks against evolving threats: A member of the organization might dissent from the report if they have substantive concerns about the long-term effectiveness and survivability of Marine Tanks against potential threats posed by countries like North Korea, Russia, and China. They may argue that advancements in anti-tank weaponry, including advanced missile systems and unmanned vehicles, could render tanks less relevant or even obsolete in future conflicts.

Disagreement with prioritizing tank deployments in certain regions: The dissenter may take issue with the document's emphasis on current tank deployments in Afghanistan and potential threats from countries like North Korea, Russia, and China. They might contend that allocating resources to these regions takes away from more pressing priorities or fails to adequately address emerging threats elsewhere. Their principled dissent could stem from a different strategic perspective or regional focus within the organization.

Overall, a member of the organization responsible for this document might dissent due to differing views on the effectiveness of tanks in specific combat environments, concerns about their relevance in certain operational contexts, doubts about their future viability against evolving threats, or disagreement with the prioritization of tank deployments in certain regions. These principled and substantive reasons may lead to dissenting opinions within the organization's assessment of Marine Tank performance and capabilities.

## RED TEAM CRITIQUE

Overall, this document provides a comprehensive overview of the performance and capabilities of Marine Tanks in various combat environments. However, there are some areas that require further analysis and consideration.

Firstly, while the document highlights the success of Marine Tanks in high kinetic conventional fights such as the Gulf War and the invasion of Iraq in 2003, it does not adequately address any limitations or weaknesses observed during these operations. This lack of critical assessment may create an unrealistic perception of invincibility surrounding Marine Tanks.

Moreover, when discussing unconventional high intensity environments like the Battle of Fallujah, the document only mentions their success without delving into specific tactics or strategies employed by tanks to overcome challenges unique to urban warfare. A more detailed analysis would benefit readers by providing insights into how tanks effectively operated within an urban environment.

The document briefly touches upon tank operations in low intensity environments like Somalia but fails to explore potential limitations that might arise from operating tanks in humanitarian missions. It would be valuable to discuss any logistical difficulties faced by tanks when conducting humanitarian operations and whether there are instances where alternative platforms might be more suitable for such tasks.

While emphasizing offensive capability, survivability, and firepower is important for showcasing tank superiority, it would be beneficial to also include information on defensive measures taken against anti-tank weapons utilized by modern adversaries. Examining lessons learned from previous engagements with anti-tank systems will provide a more complete understanding of current vulnerabilities and existing countermeasures.

Additionally, although mentioning current deployments in Afghanistan is relevant, there should be further discussion regarding specific roles and contributions made by Marine Tanks in this particular conflict zone. Understanding their effectiveness within the context of Afghanistan will enhance readers' understanding of their capabilities under different operational circumstances.

Lastly, identifying potential threats posed by countries like North Korea, Russia, and China is essential; however, expanding on these threats with a thorough assessment of adversary capabilities would add greater depth to this section. Evaluating how well-equipped Marine Tanks are to counter specific threats from these countries, including potential technological advancements and tactics, will provide a more accurate evaluation of their future effectiveness.

In conclusion, while the document covers various aspects of Marine Tanks' performance and capabilities in different combat environments, it would benefit from a more critical analysis of limitations observed during past operations. Additionally, further exploration of tank operations in unconventional and low intensity environments, as well as detailed assessments of defensive measures against anti-tank weapons and adversary capabilities would enhance the comprehensiveness of this document.

## MAGA PERSPECTIVE

This document is nothing more than liberal propaganda aimed at glorifying Marine Tanks and downplaying their shortcomings. While it may highlight their success in certain combat environments, it conveniently ignores the numerous failures and inefficiencies that have plagued these tanks in the past.

First of all, the document fails to mention the significant cost associated with maintaining and operating Marine Tanks. These machines are incredibly expensive to build, maintain, and repair, draining valuable resources from other important areas of our military budget. It is irresponsible to continue investing in tanks when there are more cost-effective and technologically advanced options available.

Furthermore, the document only focuses on a handful of instances where Marine Tanks were successful. This cherry-picking of examples creates a false narrative that these tanks are always effective. In reality, there have been countless instances where they have been outmaneuvered or rendered useless by modern warfare tactics such as drone strikes or guerrilla warfare.

Additionally, the document seems to suggest that Marine Tanks are necessary for supporting the Marine Air Ground Task Force. This is an outdated notion that ignores the advancements in military technology. With the rise of unmanned aerial vehicles and precision-guided missiles, tanks are becoming increasingly obsolete on the battlefield.

Lastly, the document unnecessarily stokes fear by mentioning potential threats from countries like North Korea, Russia, and China. This fear-mongering tactics is typical of liberal elites who want us to believe that we need to constantly increase our military presence around the world. In reality, diplomacy and economic cooperation should be prioritized over spending billions on tanks that serve little purpose in modern warfare.

In conclusion, this document serves as nothing more than a biased attempt to justify continued investment in Marine Tanks. The information it provides is skewed and incomplete, failing to acknowledge the flaws and inefficiencies inherent in these machines. It is time to reassess our priorities and invest in more effective and cost-efficient means of defense.

# PAGE-BY-PAGE SUMMARIES

*BODY-1*   This page is a report on the offensive capability of Marine Tanks in the Marine Air Ground Task Force, highlighting their importance as America's middle-weight fighting force. It emphasizes the need for the Marine Corps to maintain a dedicated tank capability despite budget constraints.

*BODY-2*   Instructions for completing SF 298, a form used to provide information about a report, including the report date, type, title, contract and grant numbers, author(s), organization name and address, sponsor/monitor information, distribution statement, abstract, subject terms, security classification, and limitation of abstract.

*BODY-3*   This page is a title page for a Master's thesis on Marine tanks and their role as America's middle-weight fighting force.

*BODY-4*   The Marine Corps Tank Community possesses superior ability to be the hard punch of the United States Marine Corps as America's middle-weight fighting force, despite potential future challenges and changing warfare environments.

*BODY-6*   The author expresses their admiration for the Marine Corps Tank Community and discusses the reduction of tank units in the Marine Corps. They argue that maintaining a viable tank capability is important for the Marine Corps' ability to effectively engage in high-intensity conflicts. The author thanks their family and various individuals who supported them throughout their research.

*BODY-7*   The page provides an overview of the use of marine tanks in different combat environments, including high kinetic fights, unconventional high intensity battles, and low intensity situations. It also discusses future improvements to support the marine tank fight.

*BODY-8*   The Marine Corps Tank Community has demonstrated superior offensive capability and is seen as the heavy punch of the United States Marine Corps. The success in previous conflicts highlights the importance of tanks in the MAGTF concept.

*BODY-9*   Marine Tank units have demonstrated their ability to provide firepower and maneuverability in various conflicts, including the 1991 Gulf War and operations in Somalia. Despite scrutiny, they continue to support the Marine Corps' mission effectively.

*BODY-10*  This page discusses the role of Marine Tank units in both high intensity and low intensity situations, highlighting their contributions during the Battle of Fallujah and Operation Restore Hope. It also mentions the denial of requested armor reinforcements and the potential impact on the Battle of Mogadishu. The page concludes by discussing technological upgrades and improvements in tank team employment for future success.

*BODY-11*  Marine Infantry and Tankers trained together in simulated combat scenarios to refine their tactics and techniques. This training proved invaluable during the 1991 Gulf War, demonstrating the superior capability of US tanks and crewmen against Iraqi opponents.

*BODY-12*  The M1A1 tank proved its worth in combat during the Gulf War, providing overwhelming firepower and superior performance for US forces. It breached Iraqi minefields, moved at high speeds, and survived enemy fire without any losses. American tank units demonstrated their power and precision in destroying enemy armored vehicles.

*BODY-13*  Marine and Army tanks demonstrated superior firepower and maneuverability in the invasions of Kuwait in 1991 and Iraq in 2003, effectively destroying enemy forces with minimal casualties.

BODY-14    Tanks provided essential protection and situational awareness in the 2003 invasion
           of Iraq, allowing for aggressive attacks and gathering information on enemy forces.
           Their strong armor made them the preferred choice for leading the fight.

BODY-15    American ground commanders showcased the effectiveness of long-range precision
           firepower and speed in conventional campaigns, proving that the Marine Corps could
           hold its own despite being numerically inferior. Tanks played a crucial role in these
           campaigns. In the Battle for Fallujah, tank units faced challenges in an urban
           environment against insurgent forces.

BODY-16    American tanks proved effective in the urban environment during the 2003 attack on
           Fallujah. Tank and infantry teams worked together to clear the city of enemy forces,
           using precision firepower to minimize collateral damage. Their coordination and
           innovative techniques allowed them to operate effectively as a unit.

BODY-17    Marine Corps tanks proved to be a powerful force in the Battle for Fallujah,
           showcasing their effectiveness in urban warfare. Tanks were also successful in low-
           intensity operations in Somalia, demonstrating their versatility and impact in
           different conflict environments.

BODY-18    The page discusses the effectiveness of tanks in supporting infantry units and
           providing security for humanitarian aid in Somalia. It also mentions the potential
           impact of having more tanks during the Battle of Mogadishu.

BODY-19    The page discusses the resource shortfall in available armor forces during the U.S.
           operations in Somalia, which resulted in the inability to rescue U.S. Army Rangers
           under intense hostile fire. The initial force sent to Somalia was significant in size and
           capability but lacked important assets.

BODY-20    The page discusses the impact of the United States military intervention in Somalia,
           specifically focusing on the efforts to support humanitarian convoys and neutralize
           enemy clans. The presence of the coalition forces increased rapidly in violent areas to
           ensure relief efforts could proceed.

BODY-21    The page discusses the use of tanks and heavy weapons in a dangerous and combat-
           like humanitarian environment in Mogadishu. The tanks were often used as a bluff
           due to the lack of appropriate ammunition, but their reputation for superior
           survivability and precision application was well-known. When necessary, the tanks
           and heavy weapons were highly effective against the opposition.

BODY-22    The use of tanks in low intensity conflict scenarios provides superior armor protection
           and allows for confident target identification. In one instance, a tank platoon
           commander chose not to engage a potential enemy tank, which turned out to be
           children playing in an unserviceable tank. The use of tanks prevents potential
           friendly fire incidents and mitigates negative public support.

BODY-23    The M1A1 tank's superior lethality, survivability, and mobility make it a top choice
           among main battle tanks. Its presence alone instills fear and intimidation in
           potential enemies, as observed by American troops in Somalia. Critics may dismiss
           this notion, but the development of countermeasures against tanks suggests
           otherwise.

BODY-24    The M1A1 tank provided psychological and physical advantage, allowing the infantry
           to maintain control and dissuade attacks in Somalia. Armor was used whenever
           possible, with a reserve maintained for potential trouble spots. Marine Tanks
           demonstrated effective operation in both high and low conflict situations.

BODY-25    The humanitarian operation in Somalia in 1992-1994 initially succeeded but
           deteriorated after the Marines withdrew, leading to the Battle of Mogadishu. The

investigation concluded that the denial of armor reinforcements contributed to the disastrous outcome and could have saved lives.

BODY-26  Denying the request for additional forces during the Battle of Mogadishu was a mistake, leading to the failure of the United States mission in Somalia. Marine Tanks have proven to be a valuable asset in various conflicts and continue to seek improvements in equipment and training techniques.

BODY-27  The Marine Tank community provides heavy lethal capability as an independent force and supports infantry units. Upgrades to the M1A1 tank have improved its ability to identify and engage targets at greater ranges. The tank commander can now engage enemy targets beyond 4000 meters with the assistance of enhanced electronics. The tank is a more lethal tool for the MAGTF and can support infantry operations in clearing urban areas and trench-lines.

BODY-28  Marine tanks are being used to support infantry in unconventional warfare, providing superior armor protection and fire support. They have been successful in Iraq and are now being deployed in Afghanistan despite some criticism.

BODY-29  American forces have utilized tanks from allied countries in the Afghan Theater, including Canadian Leopard 2's and Danish tanks. The move to deploy American tanks to Afghanistan is seen as necessary for protecting troops and closing in on the enemy while protecting civilian populations. The Marine Corps' Tank community must continue to refine its operations and acknowledge the ongoing threat of large-scale conventional engagements.

BODY-30  North Korea has deployed a new battle tank, named "Pokpung-Ho," based on the Soviet-built T-72, and has increased its number of tanks to about 4,100. Russia also poses a threat with their strong offensive armor capability demonstrated during the invasion of Georgia. They have made improvements to their tanks, including a larger main gun and upgraded technology.

BODY-31  The page discusses Russia's efforts to match American tank technology and the potential implications of their ability to mass produce equipment. It also mentions China's development of main battle tanks and their aggressive pursuit of global power.

BODY-32  China has made significant advancements in tank production, focusing on speed, target identification, main gun lethality, and armor protection. They are also improving their fire control system and threat identification capabilities. China is pursuing offensive power with improved engines and a new tank main gun. These developments highlight China's commitment to achieving military strength on the ground.

BODY-33  The page discusses the importance of maintaining a strong offensive capability in the Marine Corps, specifically in the tank community, despite the predominant threat being from unconventional forces. It argues that high intensity conflict is still a possibility and that the Marine Corps should maintain an extremely powerful armor offensive capability to operate effectively in any theater of operation.

BODY-34  The page discusses the importance of maintaining a superior military capability and the effectiveness of Marine Tanks in past battles.

BODY-36  This page is a bibliography of various sources related to tanks and military operations, including lessons learned from Somalia operations, the use of tanks in Route Security, and the effectiveness of tanks in Operation Iraqi Freedom.

# NOTABLE PASSAGES

BODY-1    *"Though the world is in a constant state of change and today's environment might suggest a conventional conflict is not strongly probable. The stance of this paper is that our Nation and Corps must always be prepared to operate in the conventional arena. The Marine Corps might not be a fully mechanized armor tank force, and fiscal constraints threaten to continue whittling away at the conventional strength within the Corps ranks. It still should continue to maintain a dedicated tank capability it can always have at its disposal to integrate into the MAGTF to ensure future battlefield success in any non-permissive future environment."*

BODY-4    *"Though the world is in a constant state of change and today's environment might suggest a conventional conflict is not strongly probable. Our Nation and Corps must always be prepared to operate in the conventional arena."*

BODY-6    *"My fear is that with this trend the pendulum is swinging dangerously too far to the low intensity side of the conflict continuum, and if the Marine Corps wants to maintain the ability to effect the high side of conflict as America's middle-weight fighter, it must maintain a viable tank capability that can be employed with the Marine Air Ground Task Force (MAGTF). Ultimately, I chose my topic in an effort to remind readers of the positive contributions Marine Tanks have provided the Corps on the battlefield in a wide range of combat scenarios in recent past, and that they stand ready for continued service as part of the finest fighting team on any battlefield in the future."*

BODY-8    *"In today's chaotic world with the great degree of regional instability throughout the globe, the Marine Corps is still expected by the people of the United States and their leaders to be America's force in readiness, able to operate in every spectrum of conflict and be able to carry the day."*

BODY-9    *"In essence Marine Tanks continually provided the heavy-handed punch to any adversarial force that wished to contest the mission accomplishment of the Marine Corps throughout the past two plus decades."*

BODY-10    *"Finally, it will provide thoughts on how recent new technological upgrades to Marine Tanks and improvements in infantry~ tank team employment have set the stage for future success on any battlefield the United States Marines might find themselves on, whether the situation offers a regular or irregular threat scenario."*

BODY-11    *"The 1991 Gulf War was an early event over the past two decades that validated this training methodology. It further demonstrated the superior capability of the armor-available to United States, and more importantly the superior ability of the. United States tank crewmen in the execution of their armor tactics and tank gunnery skills against their Iraqi opponents."*

BODY-12    *"In battle the MlAl provided United States forces overwhelming firepower that established offensive dominance over Iraq units. Breaching through the minefields emplaced by Iraqi forces, Marine Tank units made an aggressive march to the north that allowed Marine Forces to seize the offensive initiative and momentum throughout the entire campaign."*

BODY-13    *"In both of these highly kinetic scenarios the ~anks of Marine and Army units demonstrated the superior firepower, maneuverability and lethality America.n fighting forces have come to expect from its heavy annor units. The MlAl Tank showed in each campaign that it maintains a superior ability to withstand enemy direct fire."*

BODY-14 "Tanks were essential because situational awareness regarding enemy forces was poor at the regimental/brigade level and below. While operational-level commanders often had enough situational awareness to meet their needs, tactical commanders need a degree of detail that was rarely available. As a result, there was constant danger of encountering the enemy without warning. Since the tanks could survive hits from a concealed enemy; they were the weapons of choice for the 'tip of the spear.' Indeed, this operation demonstrated the inverse relationship between force protection and situation awareness."

BODY-15 "In each account of these conventional campaigns the United States showcased to the world that though the Marine Corps may be numerically inferior to many organizations it may meet on the battlefield, it could more than hold its own. The MAGTF concept was not only validated in each campaign, but proved to be an integral part of the United States maneuver warfare prowess. Vital to the success of the MAGTF was the employment of Marine Tank units. They provided a great annor punch as an independent maneuver element, proving in many cases to be the decisive element on the field of battle. Marine Tanks had been tested and had earned high marks for their conventional.success."

BODY-16 "The Infantry-Tank integrated teams of Marine units operated seamlessly together to methodically clear the entire city of enemy forces. Tanks providing precision firepower maximized effects on enemy while preventing undesired collateral damage in the loss of innocent civilian life. The tank provided a sole ability to support infantry assault forces in breaching obstacles and building walls. Additionally, with the precision of the tank main gun, the tank proved vital to moving into firing position with relative safety and reducing enemy strong points."

BODY-17 "The Marines who fought in Fallujah made a profound statement to potential enemy forces throughout the world. The tank was not just an asset to fight other tanks, but a platform that, when integrated with the infantry team, is a lethal force against those who think they can dig in and hide in the urban terrain."

BODY-18 "The campaign that highlight the effective employment of tanks supporting infantry units in establishment of positive security conditions that allowed transit of humanitarian aid to the suffering populace."

BODY-19 "This refusal received wide public attention in light of the catastrophic events that transpired during 3-4 October of 1993 when U.S. Army Rangers came under intense hostile fire and it rapidly became clear that the Quick Reaction Force lacked the capability to rescue them."

BODY-20 "Those adversarial armed groups no longer held the operational advantage they had enjoyed for quite some time. They now had to make a decision, either retreat into the landscape in an attempt to wait out the humanitarian effort that had been launched, or attempt to fight it out with the humanitarian coalition force."

BODY-21 "The reputation of the MlAl's superior survivability, capability and superior precision application of its small arms was well known by the commanders on the ground. The commanders employed this fact with great effe~tiveness and though the Americans posse~sed a superior lethal· land based weapons capability they were very conscious to use discretion when putting armor into play. Heavy weapons were used as a last resort, however, in the instances when they were necessary (e.g. in action against a warlord's compound), the tanks and heavy weapons were highly effective, reinforced by the fact the opposition had nothing to match them."

BODY-22   *"The tank provided the commander a moment of pause for he possessed the confidence the unmatched lethality and survivability the M1A1 provided. If a lesser vehicle had responded the outcome could very well have been different."*

BODY-23   *"The tank's great size and speed; its weapons, and the loud noises it makes all seemed to very much intimidate any potential trouble-makers, in short, when armor moved in the bandits moved out."*

BODY-24   *"The existence of the M1A1 tank... provided '... as much psychological as physical advantage for the infantry. It allowed the infantry to be much more accepting of the restricted ROE (Rules of Engagement) and dissuaded the hostile elements from attacking CTJF(Combined Joint Task Force). The forces that were the most protected and best armed were most able to maintain control of the operational environment and maintain the initiative thereby imprinting their will upon the populace."*

BODY-25   *"The congressional report concluded tanks may have saved U.S. lives and reduced casualties?6 A reaction force supported with armor assets, including tanks, could have effectively breached obstacles and brought overwhelming fire support, establishing direct fire dominance on the enemy with a survivable platform capable of delivering persistent over-watch to American ground forces to cover the recovery of equipment and extraction of personnel."*

BODY-26   *"The tank was the single most important ground combat weapon in the war. Tanks led the advance, compensated for poor situational awareness, survived hostile fire, and terrorized the enemy. These attributes contributed much to the rapid rate of advance from Kuwait to Baghdad."*

BODY-27   *"It is difficult to believe but the Marine Tank of today is an even more lethal tool for the MAGTF on the high end of conflict than ever before. The armored combined arms maneuver support that Marine Tank Battalion's can provide is more capable and lethal than ever before."*

BODY-28   *"The Tank's ability to provide persistent over-watch and precision direct fire exceeds all other supporting arms. This ability allowed for tanks throughout the Iraq campaign to be that constant presence with the infantry that reinforced a great message of strength and provided a capability that gave dismounted personnel confidence in a very uncertain environment."*

BODY-29   *"\Vhat the mobile, protective firepower of a tank allows you to do is obviously protect your own troops, but also to take more risk to close with the enemy while protecting civilian populations".*

BODY-30   *"Most individuals remember what happened in 1950 and the sight of North Korean Tanks moving quickly south is not a sight anyone wants to see, but the prospect is not off any planning tables, it seems."*

BODY-31   *"Russia's ability to mass produce equipment for its own use, or its willingness to sell equipment to those who have not been overly friendly with the United States. These points should encourage military leaders to revisit the efforts of Russian tank development during World War II and consider how the mass production efforts of the T-34 provided the leverage for Russian armor units to defeat the technologically superior German Panther along the Eastern front."*

BODY-32   *"In pursuit of offensive power China has already begun mass production of improved 1,500 horsepower engine to propel their tanks at faster speeds, and successfully tested a new 140 millimeter tank main gun that could appear on newer models of their main battle tanks in the near future. China has made huge strides in technology, space, cyber, and industrial production capability. All of these developments point toward a* nation that understands it must be able to achieve decisive military strength in any arena."

BODY-33  "If the Marine Corps wishes to operate throughout the entire spectrum of conflict, it is the belief of this author that the Corps must maintain an extremely powerful armor offensive capability. The Marine Corps will never, and should never, seek to just fill the roles of a second land army. However, if the Corps is serious about being a true middle weight force that can respond to a wide variety of conflict and be successful then it must maintain a wide array of combat capability that can be tailored to the mission and executed through the MAGTF concept in any theater of operation."

BODY-34  "The Marine Corps should refrain from the thought tl).at large scale conventional possibilities are completely extinct and ensure the capability to compete with a conventional enemy is maintained. Marine Tanks have proven themselves a decisive punch on past battlefields and continue to stand ready to deploy in any integrated·capacity, from platoon to battalion, to provide fut':lre.MAGTFs the big punch to America's middle weight fighting force."

# REPORT DOCUMENTATION PAGE

**Form Approved**
**OMB No. 0704-0188**

| 1. REPORT DATE (DD-MM-YYYY) | 2. REPORT TYPE | 3. DATES COVERED (From - To) |
|---|---|---|
| 25-04-2011 | Master of Military Studies Research Paper | September 2010 - April 2011 |

| 4. TITLE AND SUBTITLE | | |
|---|---|---|
| Marine Tanks: The Hard Punch of America's Middle-Weight Fighting Force. | **5a. CONTRACT NUMBER** N/A | |
| | **5b. GRANT NUMBER** N/A | |
| | **5c. PROGRAM ELEMENT NUMBER** N/A | |

| 6. AUTHOR(S) | |
|---|---|
| Major Jared R. Duff, Tank Officer, United States Marine Corps | **5d. PROJECT NUMBER** N/A |
| | **5e. TASK NUMBER** N/A |
| | **5f. WORK UNIT NUMBER** N/A |

| 7. PERFORMING ORGANIZATION NAME(S) AND ADDRESS(ES) | 8. PERFORMING ORGANIZATION REPORT NUMBER |
|---|---|
| USMC Command and Staff College<br>Marine Corps University<br>2076 South Street<br>Quantico, VA 22134-5068 | N/A |

| 9. SPONSORING/MONITORING AGENCY NAME(S) AND ADDRESS(ES) | 10. SPONSOR/MONITOR'S ACRONYM(S) |
|---|---|
| N/A | N/A |
| | **11. SPONSORING/MONITORING AGENCY REPORT NUMBER** N/A |

**12. DISTRIBUTION AVAILABILITY STATEMENT**
Unlimited

**13. SUPPLEMENTARY NOTES**
N/A

**14. ABSTRACT**
This paper annotates that the demonstrated offensive capability of Marine Tanks integrated into the Marine Air Ground Task Force (MAGTF) concept, combined with recent tactical and technical developments in training and equipment, has ensured the Marine Corps Tank Community possesses superior ability to be the hard punch of the United States Marine Corps as America's middle-weight fighting force. Though the world is in a constant state of change and today's environment might suggest a conventional conflict is not strongly probable. The stance of this paper is that our Nation and Corps must always be prepared to operate in the conventional arena. The Marine Corps might not be a fully mechanized armor tank force, and fiscal constraints threaten to continue whittling away at the conventional strength within the Corps ranks. It still should to continue to maintain a dedicated tank capability it can always have at its disposal to integrate into the MAGTF to ensure future battlefield success in any non-permissive future environment.

**15. SUBJECT TERMS**
-Historical analysis of the Marine Corps M1A1 tank and Tank Units from 1990-2010.
-Analysis of current Marine Corps M1A1 Tank and Tank Unit performance on today's battlefield.
-Potential enemy armor research, development and production.
-Marine Tank units demonstrated battlefield success and abilty to continue to positively affect future battlefields.

| 16. SECURITY CLASSIFICATION OF: | | | 17. LIMITATION OF ABSTRACT | 18. NUMBER OF PAGES | 19a. NAME OF RESPONSIBLE PERSON |
|---|---|---|---|---|---|
| | | | UU | 34 | Marine Corps University / Command and Staff College |
| **a. REPORT** Unclass | **b. ABSTRACT** Unclass | **c. THIS PAGE** Unclass | | | **19b. TELEPONE NUMBER (Include area code)** (703) 784-3330 (Admin Office) |

Standard Form 298 (Rev. 8-98)
Prescribed by ANSI-Std Z39-18

# INSTRUCTIONS FOR COMPLETING SF 298

**1. REPORT DATE.** Full publication date, including day, month, if available. Must cite at lest the year and be Year 2000 compliant, e.g., 30-06-1998; xx-08-1998; xx-xx-1998.

**2. REPORT TYPE.** State the type of report, such as final, technical, interim, memorandum, master's thesis, progress, quarterly, research, special, group study, etc.

**3. DATES COVERED.** Indicate the time during which the work was performed and the report was written, e.g., Jun 1997 - Jun 1998; 1-10 Jun 1996; May - Nov 1998; Nov 1998.

**4. TITLE.** Enter title and subtitle with volume number and part number, if applicable. On classified documents, enter the title classification in parentheses.

**5a. CONTRACT NUMBER.** Enter all contract numbers as they appear in the report, e.g. F33615-86-C-5169.

**5b. GRANT NUMBER.** Enter all grant numbers as they appear in the report, e.g. 1F665702D1257.

**5c. PROGRAM ELEMENT NUMBER.** Enter all program element numbers as they appear in the report, e.g. AFOSR-82-1234.

**5d. PROJECT NUMBER.** Enter al project numbers as they appear in the report, e.g. 1F665702D1257; ILIR.

**5e. TASK NUMBER.** Enter all task numbers as they appear in the report, e.g. 05; RF0330201; T4112.

**5f. WORK UNIT NUMBER.** Enter all work unit numbers as they appear in the report, e.g. 001; AFAPL30480105.

**6. AUTHOR(S).** Enter name(s) of person(s) responsible for writing the report, performing the research, or credited with the content of the report. The form of entry is the last name, first name, middle initial, and additional qualifiers separated by commas, e.g. Smith, Richard, Jr.

**7. PERFORMING ORGANIZATION NAME(S) AND ADDRESS(ES).** Self-explanatory.

**8. PERFORMING ORGANIZATION REPORT NUMBER.** Enter all unique alphanumeric report numbers assigned by the performing organization, e.g. BRL-1234; AFWL-TR-85-4017-Vol-21-PT-2.

**9. SPONSORING/MONITORS AGENCY NAME(S) AND ADDRESS(ES).** Enter the name and address of the organization(s) financially responsible for and monitoring the work.

**10. SPONSOR/MONITOR'S ACRONYM(S).** Enter, if available, e.g. BRL, ARDEC, NADC.

**11. SPONSOR/MONITOR'S REPORT NUMBER(S).** Enter report number as assigned by the sponsoring/ monitoring agency, if available, e.g. BRL-TR-829; -215.

**12. DISTRIBUTION/AVAILABILITY STATEMENT.** Use agency-mandated availability statements to indicate the public availability or distribution limitations of the report. If additional limitations/restrictions or special markings are indicated, follow agency authorization procedures, e.g. RD/FRD, PROPIN, ITAR, etc. Include copyright information.

**13. SUPPLEMENTARY NOTES.** Enter information not included elsewhere such as: prepared in cooperation with; translation of; report supersedes; old edition number, etc.

**14. ABSTRACT.** A brief (approximately 200 words) factual summary of the most significant information.

**15. SUBJECT TERMS.** Key words or phrases identifying major concepts in the report.

**16. SECURITY CLASSIFICATION.** Enter security classification in accordance with security classification regulations, e.g. U, C, S, etc. If this form contains classified information, stamp classification level on the top and bottom of this page.

**17. LIMITATION OF ABSTRACT.** This block must be completed to assign a distribution limitation to the abstract. Enter UU (Unclassified Unlimited) or SAR (Same as Report). An entry in this block is necessary if the abstract is to be limited.

*United States Marine Corps*
*Command and Staff College*
*Marine Corps University*
*2076 South Street*
*Marine Corps Combat Development Command*
*Quantico, Virginia 22134-5068*

MASTER OF MILITARY STUDIES

---

**TITLE:**
MARINE TANKS:
THE HARD PUNCH OF AMERICA'S MIDDLE-WEIGHT FIGHTING FORCE.

SUBMITTED IN PARTIAL FULFILLMENT
OF THE REQUIRMENTS FOR THE DEGREE OF
MASTER OF MILITARY STUDIES.

**AUTHOR:**
MAJOR JARED R. DUFF, TANK OFFICER, UNITED STATES MARINE CORPS.

AY 10-11

---

Mentor and Oral Defense Committee Member: Dr. *Bradley J. Meyer, Ph.D*
Approved: *Bradley J. Meyer*
Date: *25 April 2011*

Oral Defense Committee Member: *Donald F. Bittner, Ph.D*
Approved: *[signature]*
Date: *25 April 2011*

# Executive Summary

**Title:** Marine Tanks: The Hard Punch of America's Middle-Weight Fighting Force.

**Author:** Major Jared R. Duff, Tank Officer, United States Marine Corps

**Thesis:** The demonstrated offensive capability of Marine Tanks integrated into the Marine Air Ground Task Force (MAGTF) concept, combined with recent tactical and technical developments in training and equipment, has ensured the Marine Corps Tank Community possesses superior ability to be the hard punch of the United States Marine Corps as America's middle-weight fighting force.

**Discussion:** The Marine Corps has continually demonstrated superior warfighting capability on the battlefield in a wide variety of combat environments. Integrating all assets available in its ranks with the MAGTF the Corps has defeated a number of adversaries, from capable enemy conventional forces to irregular threats in an unconventional setting. The M1A1 Tank of the Marine Corps has been a vital part of this battlefield success.

An ever changing world that calls into question the potential of large scale conventional conflict combined with ever tightening fiscal constraints faced by the Marine Corps place the future of the M1A1 in peril. Many military professionals are solely focused on the irregular fights that the United States has faced as a nation in the recent past. The movement towards an ever lighter and civilian integrated force has full momentum going into the future. Though this is a very real consideration that must be planned and prepared for, the Corps must not fall into the trap of planning to fight the last war. If the Corps does so, it could very possibly leave the Corps, and Nation, vulnerable to a future attempt by a rising nation state seeking to decisively defeat the United States on an asymmetrical battlefield that was weighted heavily towards the conventional end of the conflict continuum.

Though recent past and current operational theaters have shown a propensity for the combat environment to lean toward the low intensity unconventional portion of the conflict continuum, there will always remain the possibility for a foreign belligerent to operate in the conventional environment. Recent trends observed in current tank development and production efforts by a number of countries, with historically adversarial attitudes toward the United States, bring about valid concerns with regards to the United States ability to maintain an adequately capable conventional force. The United States Marine Corps must never forget its promise to the American people to remain the United States' armed force in readiness. This entails having a balanced force that is able to operate effectively along the entire continuum of conflict from the unconventional to the conventional, as stated by the current Commandant of the Marine Corps General James Amos.

**Conclusion:** Though the world is in a constant state of change and today's environment might suggest a conventional conflict is not strongly probable. Our Nation and Corps must always be prepared to operate in the conventional arena. The Marine Corps might not be a fully mechanized armor tank force, and fiscal constraints threaten to continue whittling away at the conventional strength within the Corps ranks. It still should maintain a dedicated tank capability it can always have at its disposal to integrate into the MAGTF to ensure future battlefield success in any non-permissive future environment.

DISCLAIMER

THE OPINIONS AND CONCLUSION EXPRESSED HEREIN ARE THOSE OF THE
INDIVIDUAL STUDENT AUTHOR AND DO NOT NECESSARILY REPRESENT THE
VIEWS OF EITHER THE MARINE CORPS COMMAND AND STAFF COLLEGE OR ANY
OTHER GOVERNMENT AGENCY. REFERENCES TO THIS STUDY SHOULD
INCLUDE THE FOREGOING STATEMENT.

QUOTATION FROM, ABSTRACTION FROM, OR REPRODUCTION OF ALL OR ANY
PART OF THIS DOCUMENT IS PERMITTED PROVIDED PROPER
ACKNOWLEDGMENT IS MADE.

## *Preface*

I have had the privilege and pleasure of serving my country of the United States and its Marine Corps as a Tank Officer. Throughout my service I have been honored to have served under the command of truly great leaders and mentors, whom I have come to idolize and respect in the greatest degree. My admiration for the hard work ethic and dedicated professionalism of the enlisted men I have led in the tank community has grown exponentially with every new position I have had the fortune of being assigned. The experience of working with these great men of the Marine Corps Tank Community, and the decorated history of the tank units throughout the Corps past, bring me an extreme level of pride to be a part of its community. Commanding Marine Corps M1A1 Tank units at the Platoon and Company level have been the proudest moments in my life. This source of pride and commitment encouraged my focus in pursuit of a Master's Thesis topic in an attempt to positively contribute to the further development of equipment, tactics, techniques and procedures of the Tank Community in its support to Marine Infantry.

Despite the battlefield success over the past two decades accomplished by Marine Tank units, the Marine Corps experienced a significant reduction of its tank force. After Operations Desert Shield and Desert Storm in 1991 the Marine Corps cased the colors of 3rd Tank Battalion, leaving in its ranks only two active duty and two reserve tank battalions. Then following the success of the initial invasion of Iraq, the reserve tank battalion of 8th Tanks was removed from the Corps Ranks. Finally, with the recent published Marine Corps Force Structure Review of 2011, the Corps has initiated the deactivation of an additional 20% of its Tank units. Recent changes with the United States' potential adversary forces around the globe, combined with fiscal constraints across the spectrum of government have contributed to this trend. My fear is that with this trend the pendulum is swinging dangerously too far to the low intensity side of the conflict continuum, and if the Marine Corps wants to maintain the ability to effect the high side of conflict as America's middle-weight fighter, it must maintain a viable tank capability that can be employed with the Marine Air Ground Task Force (MAGTF). Ultimately, I chose my topic in an effort to remind readers of the positive contributions Marine Tanks have provided the Corps on the battlefield in a wide range of combat scenarios in recent past, and that they stand ready for continued service as part of the finest fighting team on any battlefield in the future.

I would like to thank my wife Amanda and my Son Jared Jr. for their patience and understanding throughout this project. Special thanks are due to the wonderful support personnel at the Gray Research Center for their assistance with my research and academic writing efforts. Thank you to my academic mentor Dr. Bradley Meyer (Ph.D), School of Advanced Warfighting, for his patience and mentorship. Lastly, I would be remised if I did not thank my Civilian Faculty Advisor, Dr. Rebecca Johnson (Ph.D), for her encouragement and support; and to my Military Faculty Advisor, Colonel Mark Strong (USA) for his guidance and direction in my pursuit of this challenging endeavor. To all of you I am very grateful.

# Table of Contents

## I. Introduction

In today's chaotic world with the great degree of regional instability throughout the globe, the Marine Corps is still expected by the people of the United States and their leaders to be America's force in readiness, able to operate in every spectrum of conflict and be able to carry the day.[1] The current Commandant of the Marine Corps, General James Amos, has stated "in order to maintain the ability to fulfill its mission expected by America the United States Marine Corps must prepare itself similar to a middle weight fighter, light enough to move quickly into any theater of operation while maintaining the appropriate combat strength to defeat any of today's conventional threats until follow on forces arrive".[2] Every fan of boxing, or any hand to hand fighting style, understands that a middle-weight fighter is light on his feet, quick with his hands, possesses superior mental and physical toughness, while maintaining a strong knockout punch capability. In recent history the Marine Corps Tank Community has provided the Corps with a significant offensive capability. The demonstrated offensive capability of Marine Tanks integrated into the MAGTF concept, combined with recent tactical and technical developments in training and equipment, has ensured the Marine Corps Tank Community possesses superior ability to be the heavy punch of the United States Marine Corps as America's middle-weight fighting force.

Over the past two decades the United States has experienced great fortune in achieving one-sided conventional victories during two major high intensity conflicts. The first was the liberation of Kuwait from Iraq forces in 1991, and the second was the successful defeat of the Iraq Armed Forces during the United States' led coalition invasion of Iraq in 2003. In each of these contest the United States Marine Corps demonstrated superior war fighting capability with its Marine Air Ground Task Force (MAGTF) concept. Marine Tank units played a pivotal role in each conflict supporting their infantry brethren with armored shock, firepower and maneuver. In those same two decades there was a significantly larger amount of smaller middle to low intensity campaigns throughout the globe, against irregular threats of both state and non-state actors.

In each of these campaigns Marine Tank units and their crews demonstrated a great ability. They adapted to the specific operational environment, continually providing armor protected precision firepower to dismounted infantry. A great example of this capability was the ground operations in Somalia when the United States Marine Corps participated in operations to establish positive security conditions that would allow for effective humanitarian operations to take place. This ability to operate over a large portion of the continuum of conflict demonstrated the Marine Corps Tank Community's ability to provide a highly maneuverable, survivable and lethal ground combat capability to the MAGTF in any non-permissive operational environment.

In essence Marine Tanks continually provided the heavy-handed punch to any adversarial force that wished to contest the mission accomplishment of the Marine Corps throughout the past two plus decades. The Marine Corps Tank community has been under great scrutiny throughout its history due to the weight of the tank and the logistical requirements that inherently come with its operation and maintenance. Despite the continued demonstration of superior performance on every battlefield the Tank community has operated in support of the Marine Corps past missions, this scrutiny remains. There is passionate debate on both sides of thought regarding the issue of continuing the tank community in the Corps. In an effort to provide substance to the point of Marine Tanks and their continued ability to support the Corps' future mission, this document will briefly reflect on the superior performance of Marine Tank battalion's during the high intensity periods of the 1991 Gulf War, and operations supporting the United States led coalition invasion of Iraq in 2003 against a very large conventional threat. This paper will revisit the Marine Tank units operating at the company level in support of I Marine Expeditionary Force (Forward)'s efforts during the Battle of Fallujah in 2004, during a high intensity situation against an unconventional enemy. Then it will make a transition from the high intensity to the low intensity realm, taking an in depth look to recognize contributions Marine Tanks made during humanitarian operations in support of Operation Restore Hope in Somalia, 1992-1993. It will annotate a few observations on the subsequent degradation of the security environment experienced by United States forces remaining behind after the withdrawal of Marine forces, specifically how requested armor reinforcements that were denied by top leadership in the chain of command could have assisted during the tragic events during the Battle of Mogadishu on 3-4 October of 1993. Finally, it will provide thoughts on how recent new technological upgrades to Marine Tanks and improvements in infantry-tank team employment have set the stage for future success on any battlefield the United States Marines might find themselves on, whether the situation offers a regular or irregular threat scenario.

**II. Marine Tanks in the High Kinetic Conventional Fight: 1991 and 2003.**

Anyone in the military profession who hears the terms conventional and high kinetic immediately thinks of images of artillery impacting the deck, small arms tracer rounds flying through air, the sound of large caliber direct fire weapons engaging enemy targets, and aircraft populating the sky. It is the type of fight the Marine Corps prided itself on preparing to conduct. The old Combined Arms Exercises (CAX) at the Marine Air Ground Combat Center at Twentynine Palms, California was the epitome of live fire maneuver training. Every infantry battalion's greatest joy was traveling to the Mojave Desert to experience the challenge and adrenaline rush of employing infantry maneuver supported by rotary and fixed winged aircraft, indirect fire assets of mortars and large caliber artillery, and every direct fire capability from the 25 millimeter of Light Armored Reconnaissance (LAR) Vehicles to the 120 millimeter of M1A1 Main Battle Tanks. All were conducted with live ammunition under the close supervision of the controllers of the Tactical Training Exercise Control Group (TTECG) in the open desert against a simulated conventional threat. In these exercises Marine Infantry perfected their techniques of employing artillery and close air support. They refined techniques in both offensive maneuver and defense engagement area development. In these scenarios a huge learning opportunity for the battalion staff's was the employment of tank support as both a separate maneuver element in support of exploiting enemy weakness, and as an integrated fire support element when closing with and dominating an enemy defensive position. Marine Infantry relished this training opportunity. It was also the type of event that was a part of prized training coveted by Marine Tankers. Though the event was simulated, with no living belligerent in the impact area, the training was invaluable. It provided an opportunity to hone the skills required to employ combined infantry-tank tactics to the optimal level on the battlefield. This practice in tactics and technique refinement would ultimately translate to the protection of American Marine lives, while continually building upon the symbiotic relationship the Marine Infantryman and Tanker needed to guarantee future battlefield success.

The 1991 Gulf War was an early event over the past two decades that validated this training methodology. It further demonstrated the superior capability of the armor available to United States, and more importantly the superior ability of the United States tank crewmen in the execution of their armor tactics and tank gunnery skills against their Iraqi opponents. Operation Desert Storm was the first test of the M1A1 Main Battle Tank in a real world engagement scenario. Developed for offensive maneuver focused towards the plains of the European landscape against a heavily armored foe, the Soviet Union, it was the most technologically advanced ground based weapons system of the day. Though it possessed great attributes and had years of research and development behind it, the fact remained the M1A1 had yet to earn its battle credentials in real combat. The performance of the M1A1 in the Army and Marine Corps units was nothing short of breathtaking.

In battle the M1A1 provided United States forces overwhelming firepower that established offensive dominance over Iraq units. Breaching through the minefields emplaced by Iraqi forces, Marine Tank units made an aggressive march to the north that allowed Marine Forces to seize the offensive initiative and momentum throughout the entire campaign. Iraqi defenders marveled at the Americans' ability to move at a high rate of speed while maintaining a superior performance, engaging Iraqi targets on the move with deadly precision.[3] Reinforcing the Iraqi military's troubles in defending against this speed and lethality was the American tank's ability to survive enemy weapons effects. The armor protection provided to the Americans ensured that not one tank crewman was lost to enemy fire throughout the entire 100 hour period of combat operations.[4] A perfect example of this performance overmatch maintained by American forces was evident during the "Reveille Engagement" when Marines of Company B, 4th Tank Battalion made visual contact with an Iraqi Armor Column comprised of T-72 and T-55 Main Battle Tanks and Infantry Fighting Vehicles during the initial stages of the attack towards Kuwait. During this armor engagement the Marines of Company B destroyed over 40 enemy armored vehicles, including over 30 enemy tanks, in approximately twenty minutes without a single friendly vehicle lost.[5] The speed, armor protection, and direct fire precision of United States Army and Marine Corps Tank units set the precedence for the level of power and strength that would define United States ground capability well through the completion of the twentieth century and into the twenty-first.

Thirteen years later, in the very same operational area of the world, Marine Tanks would once again set a precedent in maneuver warfare that has been unmatched by any other nation in the world. This time American forces would be executing the invasion of Iraq in 2003 due to Iraq's hostile non-compliance of United Nation requirements with regards to international weapons inspectors. The attack would be the greatest movement of Marine forces across the largest territory of land in Marine Corps History. The Marine Corps accomplished this phenomenal feat in just over two weeks. Leading the way toward Bagdad for much of the duration were Marine Tanks. Just as in 1991 the Iraqi forces could not effectively stop the armor protected firepower of the American forces. In every case Marine Tank units were able to survive the weapons effects of Iraqi Tanks and Infantry Fighting Vehicles while effectively destroying Iraq targets at ranges well beyond three thousand meters. Throughout the entire offensive campaign to Bagdad American armored systems enabled the United States to close with and destroy the heavily armored and fanatically determined enemy force, often within urban terrain, with impunity.[6] This ability for American Tank units to conduct offensive operations with this extremely high degree of success was instrumental to the expedient destruction of any Iraqi unit that fought against the initial United States invasion force.

In both of these highly kinetic scenarios the tanks of Marine and Army units demonstrated the superior firepower, maneuverability and lethality American fighting forces have come to expect from its heavy armor units. The M1A1 Tank showed in each campaign that it maintains a superior ability to withstand enemy direct fire. Still maintaining a phenomenal track record of crew protection, no Army or Marine crewman died in an Abrams tank due to enemy fire penetrating the vehicle though a few American tanks were damaged by enemy fire damaging suspension systems or engine compartments that caused a few vehicle fires.[7] This level of protection instilled a great deal of confidence that promoted aggressiveness in the attack by tank units.

The level of protection not only assisted with promoting aggressiveness in the tank crewmembers, but gave ground maneuver commanders the opportunity to develop a situation on the battlefield, to ascertain the true composition and strength of the enemy. American Tank units could effectively fight for information while maintaining a sound level of safety. Many times lightly skinned vehicles of light armor or trucks in the reconnaissance role would travel forward and report on observation pertaining to enemy formations and movements. However, with the situation in Iraq during the 2003 invasion, a lot of information about the enemy's location and capability was not known. This lack of information combined with the weapons capability potential the Iraq military had available made life for reconnaissance units forward extremely hazardous. In order to mitigate the danger while maximizing battlefield opportunities, commanders on the ground put faith in the capability of their tank units to handle the task of leading forces in the fight.

> Tanks were essential because situational awareness regarding enemy forces was poor at the regimental/brigade level and below. While operational-level commanders often had enough situational awareness to meet their needs, tactical commanders need a degree of detail that was rarely available. As a result, there was constant danger of encountering the enemy without warning. Since the tanks could survive hits from a concealed enemy, they were the weapons of choice for the "tip of the spear." Indeed, this operation demonstrated the inverse relationship between force protection and situation awareness. In circumstances where situation awareness was poor, as it normally was at the brigade/regimental level and below, there was a clear need for strong armor protection forward.[8]

In this conflict American ground commanders were not only demonstrating that superior long range precision firepower combined with speed were the tools for victory, but that the ability to survive contact and fight for information was an American capability which the enemy could not match. Tanks leading the charge were effective in forcing Iraqi forces to adjust to the threat of American armor in a manner that provided the ability for American units to mass the effects of their direct fire assets, reinforced with indirect fires that spelled disaster for the enemy.

In each account of these conventional campaigns the United States showcased to the world that though the Marine Corps may be numerically inferior to many organizations it may meet on the battlefield, it could more than hold its own. The MAGTF concept was not only validated in each campaign, but proved to be an integral part of the United States maneuver warfare prowess. Vital to the success of the MAGTF was the employment of Marine Tank units. They provided a great armor punch as an independent maneuver element, proving in many cases to be the decisive element on the field of battle. Marine Tanks had been tested and had earned high marks for their conventional success.

## III. Tanks in the Unconventional High Intensity Environment: The Battle for Fallujah.

Upon declaration of the completion of combat operations in late 2003 many tank units in both the Army and Marine Corps began to transition to redeployment operations. The enemy within the borders of Iraq had different plans. In the months that followed the push to Bagdad portions of the country in the west began to experience activity by adversarial forces. This enemy activity ultimately led to a showdown between insurgent forces and United State Marines in the city of Fallujah. This fight would not be in the open spaces of desert or river basins but in the complexities of an urban environment. Opportunity presented the most challenging environment in which to fight with no two dimensional focus, but with a requirement to have

three hundred sixty degree awareness.

Though American tanks had shown that they could effectively operate in the urban

environment throughout the entire axis of attack in 2003, many critics believed that tanks would

fail in this difficult environment. The enemy had months to prepare their fighting positions and

reinforce their integrated obstacle plan to assist their defensive efforts. Despite these efforts the

heavy armor assets available to the Marines going into Fallujah provided the overwhelming

firepower and protection to push into the city. The tank elements of this force attacking the city

gave the MAGTF a capability to penetrate the enemy's defensive network. These penetrating

forces were critical to quickly slicing through the insurgents' defenses and disrupting their ability

to conduct the fight. They added significantly to the capability set of the assault force.[9]

Insurgent forces could only hope to slightly delay the inevitable.

The Infantry-Tank integrated teams of Marine units operated seamlessly together to

methodically clear the entire city of enemy forces. Tanks providing precision firepower

maximized effects on enemy while preventing undesired collateral damage in the loss of

innocent civilian life. The tank provided a solid ability to support infantry assault forces in

breeching obstacles and building walls. Additionally, with the precision of the tank main gun the

tank proved vital to moving into firing position with relative safety and reducing enemy strong

points. Marine Infantry and Tank personnel developed innovative techniques for communicating

and coordinating their efforts over small tactical radios, with hand and arm signals, and relearned

the great capability of the tank-infantry phone. Like the Marines on the island campaigns of

World War II and the Marines who fought it out with the North Vietnamese in Hue during the

Tet Offensive, tank and infantry Marines relearned to operate in complement to one another.

This symbiotic relationship revitalized a Marine Corps capability that proved to be an overwhelming power during the Battle for Fallujah, the unstoppable force of the Marine Infantry-Tank Team.

In this unconventional environment Marine Tank crewmen employed their armored platforms with great effect in the urban battlefield. Marines on the ground and in the tank redefined the capability of this armored platform, once thought too vulnerable to operate within the confines of the urban terrain. The Marines who fought in Fallujah made a profound statement to potential enemy forces throughout the world. The tank was not just an asset to fight other tanks, but a platform that, when integrated with the infantry team, is a lethal force against those who think they can dig in and hide in the urban terrain.

## IV. Tanks in the Low Intensity Environment: Somalia.

In the two previous sections performance capabilities of the M1A1 Tank were highlighted against two distinctly different enemy types. The first was against a very conventional uniformed foe that possessed their own main battle tanks, infantry fighting vehicles, artillery and additional traditional combat assets; while the second was against an unconventional threat that were not a uniformed fighting force, but a large group of insurgents with mostly small caliber weapons, some shoulder fired anti tank weapons, mortar and vehicle mounted anti-aircraft weapons. These unconventional forces used improved explosive devices and operated outside of the normal rules of modern warfare. Still, in both situations tanks were employed in a high intensity environment. On the other end of the spectrum of conflict the United States efforts to support United Nation humanitarian operations in the country of Somalia demonstrated how American Tanks could positively affect operations in the low intensity environment. This American led campaign produces learning points from the initial portions of the campaign that highlight the effective employment of tanks supporting infantry units in establishment of positive security conditions that allowed transit of humanitarian aid to the suffering populace. It shows the validity and positive contribution that Marine Tanks provided in an environment that was not saturated with enemy armor, but littered with situations that call for patience, the ability to withstand first contact, and ensuring collateral damage is kept at a minimum. Additionally, it provided thoughts to what might have been with regards to tank availability that could have reinforced the United States efforts to support the extraction of American soldiers during the Battle of Mogadishu in October of 1993.

In the early 1990s many remember the horrifying videos and pictures of dead American servicemen dragged through the streets of Mogadishu, Somalia. This disgusting scene was amplified by the hundreds of joyful and exuberant cheering Somali citizens. As the lifeless figures of these American patriots were dishonored and desecrated by the very people the United States believed they were providing assistance to, the inescapable truth of this situation was painfully evident. Security, public order and any remnants of positive control by United Nations (U.N.) Forces was not present in central Mogadishu. The United States had entered this theater of operations with honorable intentions as the lead in a U.N. humanitarian effort to ease the suffering of the Somali people from a devastating famine.

The security situation on the ground required a significant military effort to establish an environment that would allow for the required humanitarian actions to be conducted with some degree of safety by the Non-Government Organizations (NGO) and Other Government Organizations (OGA) desiring to offer assistance. As time progressed the U.N. took the lead and the U.S. withdrew a significant amount of its force from the theater, leaving behind a relatively light force for use in small direct action missions in support of the overall U.N. effort. Though this force was extremely capable it lacked important assets that would have been extremely valuable combat multipliers in support of those direct action missions. As the situation on the ground developed during this phase the on-scene commander, Major General Montgomery, identified a resource shortfall in an available armor capability to support ongoing U.S. operations. Major General Montgomery made a request for additional armor forces, including tanks, which was denied. This refusal received wide public attention in light of the catastrophic events that transpired during 3-4 October of 1993 when U.S. Army Rangers came under intense hostile fire and it rapidly became clear that the Quick Reaction Force lacked the capability to rescue them.[10]

In the beginning of the operation the United States experienced a great deal of success against the warring factions within Somalia by employing overwhelming conventional strength in the establishment of a secure environment. Upon the advice of his advisors President George H. W. Bush had decided that the United States would send in a division-sized unit under the auspices of the United Nations into the country of Somalia to provide the military assistance required in the delivery of food and other supplies.[11] This was a significant statement of commitment to the cause. On December 3, 1992 the United Nations Security Council unanimously passed Resolution 794, not only authorizing military intervention but stating that the multinational force led by the United States would be allowed to use all necessary force to accomplish its humanitarian mission.[12] The force that initially went into the country of Somalia was significant in size and capability. The forces comprised a wide variety personnel and equipment that included infantry, artillery, rotary winged aircraft (recon, assault support and attack), wheeled transportation assets, armored vehicles (infantry fighting, troop transport, recon, and tanks), along with the vast amount of logistical support capability. This had a profound effect on the armed clans operating within Somalia. Those adversarial armed groups no longer held the operational advantage they had enjoyed for quite some time. They now had to make a decision, either retreat into the landscape in an attempt to wait out the humanitarian effort that had been launched, or attempt to fight it out with the humanitarian coalition force.

Once ashore the United States Marines went to work supporting convoys transporting humanitarian supplies and food as well as neutralizing enemy clans operating in the area. One example of this effort was the formation of Task Force Mogadishu to assume security responsibilities for key facilities and to assist Force Service Support Group (FSSG) units in escorting dozens of food and military supply convoys into the interior, and to expand military presence in the many dangerous areas in and near Mogadishu.[13] Much of this security work was done patrolling on foot, establishing dialog and a presence with the people. Vital to any effort when working within an urban area is demonstrating a physical presence of commitment to prevent violent activity by any potential enemy organizations. When required this presence was reinforced with the appropriate assets in wheeled or armored assets. Though the mission of the coalition was to provide humanitarian relief to the people of Somalia, forces on the ground had a clear understanding that relief would only come if the adversarial armed clans were dealt with accordingly. Violent areas experienced a rapid increase in coalition presence from occasional patrols through saturation in a matter of weeks.[14]

As this military action by the United States Coalition continued through the initial months of these operations, the use of appropriate armed force systematically neutralized the enemy threat throughout the countryside. These military units utilized all facets of their conventional firepower capability with the appropriate rules of engagement and engagement criteria assigned to mitigate unnecessary civilian and infrastructure collateral damage. Still, much of the work was extremely difficult and dangerous work that more resembled missions in a direct combat environment rather than a humanitarian environment.

The large majority of enemy vehicle engagement was with civilian model trucks with some type of heavy machine gun or recoilless rifle mounted in the bed. Although there were tanks and artillery pieces secured in a few raids on clan weapons depots there were no direct contact engagements from enemy tank assets. The threat of heavy direct fire weapons systems of an anti armor sort was small enough that United States forces did not possess the appropriate tank main gun ammunition for issue to the Marine Tank Platoon in support of Task Force Mogadishu. In one assault on an enemy weapons depot the unit commander employing the tank platoon in support of his infantry's assault on the compound referred to his employment of the armor asset as a "bluff", believing the enemy would assume the tank's main gun would be available to the crew; however, even though no main gun ammunition was available the tanks possessed more than enough small arms ammunition for all of their mounted machine guns.[15] The reputation of the M1A1's superior survivability, capability and superior precision application of its small arms was well known by the commanders on the ground. The commanders employed this fact with great effectiveness and though the Americans possessed a superior lethal land based weapons capability they were very conscious to use discretion when putting armor into play. Heavy weapons were used as a last resort, however, in the instances when they were necessary (e.g. in action against a warlord's compound), the tanks and heavy weapons were highly effective, reinforced by the fact the opposition had nothing to match them.[16]

In addition to the direct fire capability of the tank, the thermal imaging technology available with its fire control system proved vital in proper friendly and threat identification on the battlefield, reducing potential cases of fratricide and maximizing target identification when engaging enemy forces. In one such case a U.S. Marine force with tank support employed the tank sights to positively identify a platoon-sized force of armed men as members of a Moroccan unit, potentially avoiding a friendly fire incident.[17] Utilizing the tank throughout the operating environment proved exceptionally vital to the successful neutralization of the enemy forces within the Mogadishu zone of operations. This highlights a very important capability that heavy armor brings to a low intensity conflict scenario. The superior armor protection afforded the crew allows for the men inside the tank to confidently allow a situation develop to ensure a potential target area is properly identified as a threat. One example of this is captured in the after action report submitted to Task Force Mogadishu by the tank platoon commander attached to the task force, Capt Mike Campell,

> The quick reaction force tank platoon was dispatched to a potential enemy location. Once on scene the crew quickly identified a potential enemy tank. The tank platoon commander reported back to headquarters and was subsequently given instructions to destroy the tank. The tank crew was able to observe the turret of the tank moving from side to side and the gun tube was elevating and depressing. However, there was no hostile action taking place. Once again Capt Campbell reported to higher and received the same instructions. Still, the instructions did not settle well with Capt Campbell and he chose to allow the situation to develop from the safety of his tank. By this time he had been ordered quite enthusiastically to engage the "enemy" tank. After several tense moments, three Somali children appeared from inside the turret of the tank and ran away not knowing how close they had come to being killed. The tank the children were playing in was old and unserviceable and unable to fire; the children were simply playing. The tank provided the commander a moment of pause for he possessed the confidence the unmatched lethality and survivability the M1A1 provided. If a lesser vehicle had responded the outcome could very well have been different.[18]

Imagine the headlines and potential information operations effort to mitigate potential fall out in public support with a situation involving an American unit killing three Somali children who were playing in an abandoned non-functioning abandoned tank. There is no substitute for the armor protection that the M1A1 provided and the ability to reinforce crew patience in relative safety that allowed them to positively identify and not engage a non-hostile threat in this scenario.

Superior lethality, survivability and mobility are definite trademarks of the M1A1 that ranks it top in class among main battle tank in the world. These facts bring another fine asset to any field of operation whether it is in a direct combat environment or on the other side of the conflict continuum in support of humanitarian operations: the asset of psychological intimidation. When anyone imagines what it would be like to be in the sights of a main battle tank a host of emotion and thoughts might run through their mind. The main emotion would be one of fear; at least they might attempt to empathize as to what that kind of fear would feel like. Anyone who has been in close proximity to a tank has an understanding of the sheer power the tank projects by its mere presence. The sight and sounds of a tank coming to the fight brings the emotion of sheer, unadulterated, fear combined with an undeniable personal understanding that there is little to nothing you can do to mitigate its capability and support to American infantry. This fact was observed by many American troops in Somalia, "The tank's great size and speed, its weapons, and the loud noises it makes all seemed to very much intimidate any potential trouble-makers, in short, when armor moved in the bandits moved out."[19]

Some critics denounce this point as an irrational thought. If it is in fact an irrational thought, it would be a good investigative effort to identify why so many weapons platforms in other tanks, anti-tank missiles (both vehicle mounted and ground mounted), Rocket Propelled Grenades, and air assets have received intense research and development to counter the threat of tanks on the conventional battlefield. Another point of consideration is the efforts by today's insurgent in Iraq and Afghanistan to employ larger Improvised Explosive Devices and Explosive Projectile Devices in an effort to mitigate the threat of armor. There is no denying that when a tank arrives on scene all attention is on it, due to its shear capability to deal a deadly blow to any

force that intends to harm the friendly forces in that area. The existence of the M1A1 tank

while in Somalia provided

> "... as much psychological as physical advantage for the infantry. It allowed the
> infantry to be much more accepting of the restricted ROE (Rules of Engagement) and
> dissuaded the hostile elements from attacking CTJF(Combined Joint Task Force).
> The forces that were the most protected and best armed were most able to maintain
> control of the operational environment and maintain the initiative thereby imparting
> their will upon the populace."[20]

This important advantage continued throughout the operation, and since the primary threat

continued to come from small arms fire, it made sense to employ armor whenever possible

particularly the M1A1 Tank.[21] The only constraint was that the limited number of vehicles did

not allow for employment everywhere when they were required. Because the forces available

were not always sufficient to cover all potential trouble spots, a reserve consisting of a mix of

armor was usually maintained. This way a commander could be confident that this reserve

would be adequate to prevail against any threat likely to be encountered in Somalia.[22]

Understanding the overall humanitarian nature of the mission in Somalia, leaders understood that

heavy armor units might not be required for every situation. Still, with the ever changing

security environment and operational conditions, commanders worked hard to prioritize task

assignments to optimize armor's operational contributions. Throughout this operation Marine

Tanks demonstrated awesome capability to support the MAGTF with superior visual

identification while under a significant amount of armor protection. This proved vital in

prosecution of precision direct fire that prevented unnecessary collateral damage. In Somalia

Marine Tanks had effectively proven that they could operate very effectively in both the high and

low end of the spectrum of conflict.

The humanitarian operation in Somalia in 1992-1994 undertaken by the U.N. (led initially by the U.S.) at first experienced great success at bringing required aid to thousands of starving Somali nationals. Once the Marines withdrew forces for the transition of authority to the United Nation forces, the situation on the ground immediately began to deteriorate, setting the conditions for the Battle of Mogadishu. The scheme of events directly led to the disastrous outcome of the operation and triggered a two-year investigation, culminating in a scathing critique of national security adviser Anthony Lake and Secretary of Defense Les Aspin.[23] The official reason given by Clinton Administration for denying the support requested was "U.S. policy in Somalia was to reduce its military presence...not to increase it."[24] The investigation determined that the administration rejected the request and advice to send armor reinforcements in an effort to demonstrate United States support to the United Nations' officials who were in the lead of operational control at the time of the request.[25] This armor capability shortfall at the tactical level during the Battle of Mogadishu significantly contributed to the inability of American Quick Reaction Forces on the ground to effectively reinforce and extract a Special Forces unit once enemy forces had shot down two American Black Hawk Helicopters.

The congressional report concluded tanks may have saved U.S. lives and reduced casualties.[26] A reaction force supported with armor assets, including tanks, could have effectively breached obstacles and brought overwhelming fire support, establishing direct fire dominance on the enemy with a survivable platform capable of delivering persistent over-watch to American ground forces to cover the recovery of equipment and extraction of personnel. The co-author of the report, Senator John Warner (R-Va.) made it a point to note in his comments regarding the denial of the heavy armor request; "Only compelling military - not diplomatic policy – reasons should ever be used to deny an on-scene commander such a request."[27] Though there were reasons believed by the civilian leadership of the United States not to approve the request of additional forces it is believed by many, including the author of this publication, that to deny the request was a mistake. This mistake prevented the employment of a combat asset that could have been a decisive element during the Battle of Mogadishu; ultimately history records what actually took place. The horrible events in early October 1993 ultimately set the stage for United States mission failure forcing a decision point for senior American leadership to withdraw all forces from Somalia that set the subsequent stage for the final withdraw of all forces by the United Nations.

**V. Future Improvements that will Continue to Support the Marine Tank Fight.**

Throughout history Marine Tanks have served beside their infantry brethren in every clime and place. The tank community within the Marine Corps has performed particularly well in the last two plus decades showing that it is truly an asset that can be employed by MAGTF forces in a wide array of conflicts from Low to High. In a conventional fight against a heavily armored enemy Marine M1A1s have proved exceptionally lethal at leading the way in the attack. The author of Joint Force Quarterly, Issue 39 commented, "The tank was the single most important ground combat weapon in the war. Tanks led the advance, compensated for poor situational awareness, survived hostile fire, and terrorized the enemy. These attributes contributed much to the rapid rate of advance from Kuwait to Baghdad."[28] The Marine Corps Tank community is proud of its reputation on the field of battle with its demonstrated performance and continually seeks equipment capability and the refinement of training techniques in tank employment and infantry tank integration to ensure continued superior support to the infantry it supports.

In the Marine Tank community's future it is understood that they must continue to provide two separated, yet extremely important services to the Corps; provide a heavy lethal capability as an independent armored combined arms maneuver force, and operate in direct support of infantry units as smaller integrated infantry-tank teams.[29] The Tank community will always train and operate with these two facts in mind. In a continual effort to strengthen tank capabilities to the MAGTF, over the past few years the Marine Corps has developed and implemented upgrades to the M1A1 that will increase the vehicle's lethal capability on the battlefield. One is the development of the Fire Power Enhancement Program sight that has significantly improved the tank crew's ability to identify and engage targets at much greater ranges than ever before. An additional capability this sight package provides may not directly assist the tank gunner, but assist the tank commander's ability to engage enemy targets beyond 4000 meters. Enhanced electronics will compute and display grid coordinates automatically, allowing forward observers and forward air controllers serving with tank units to call for indirect fire against targets the tank can't touch, and on radios that have been moved from the outside of the tank to the inside crew compartment, where there is protection from enemy fire.[30]

It is difficult to believe but the Marine Tank of today is an even more lethal tool for the MAGTF on the high end of conflict than ever before. The armored combined arms maneuver support that Marine Tank Battalion's can provide is more capable and lethal than ever before. In support of direct infantry operations these same assets, combined with the newly developed infantry-tank phone mounted on the tank's back deck, can be applied to tactical execution-supporting the ground commanders'' in deliberate clearing operations of both urban areas and trench-lines. These developments have increased the ability for tank crewmen and dismounted infantry to communicate, coordinate and positively destroy enemy forces while providing

maximum protection to the Marine teams.

The future trends are definitely pointing to more situations of unconventional enemies

operating in an irregular environment. The technological developments of the Marine M1A1

have set the conditions for the tank community to support its infantry brethren with superior

armor protected fire support in any environment across the spectrum of conflict. The past few

years in Iraq that followed the completion of the invasion consistently demonstrated this point.

Marine Tank units at the Platoon and Company level continually provided superior support in the

Counter Insurgency Fight. The Tank's ability to provide persistent over-watch and precision

direct fire exceeds all other supporting arms.[31] This ability allowed for tanks throughout the Iraq

campaign to be that constant presence with the infantry that reinforced a great message of

strength and provided a capability that gave dismounted personnel confidence in a very uncertain

environment.

## VI. Marine Tanks in the Current Fight.

Marine Tank capability is now being demonstrated currently in the theater of

Afghanistan, where they have supported the Marine Corps Counterinsurgency effort since

February of 2011. It is the first time since the beginning of the United States involvement in

Afghanistan that American tank units have been committed to support combat operations in

Afghan theater. It has initially met with some negative comments by some senior civilian and

military critics. Many of the arguments are very similar to the push back from critics of the

continued employment of armor units in Iraq from 2004 until the recent withdraw of American

fighting forces in 2010. Critics are leery of Afghan and international perception. Still, the fact

remains there is still very heavy fighting against enemy forces throughout the country. In many instances American forces have utilized tank forces of allied countries that have been operating in the Afghan Theater for the past few years. Canadian Leopard 2's have supported U.S. Army forces at times during offensive operations for over four years[32] The Marine Corps has utilized the services of Danish tanks in the Nawa area to reduce some hard bunkers that the Taliban had established.[33] Now Marine Tanks will be providing the service to the MAGTF as it should. Proponents of the move have stated that the tank is a necessary asset that United States forces should have at their disposal for many of the factors that have been mentioned in this article. In response to critics Brigadier General (U.S.A.) H.R. McMaster recently replied in a New York Times article as to why American Tanks should be deployed to Afghanistan: "What the mobile, protective firepower of a tank allows you to do is obviously protect your own troops, but also to take more risk to close with the enemy while protecting civilian populations".[34] This might be a sign that the nation has learned from the events of Somalia in the Battle of Mogadishu what armor and tanks bring to the lower intensity conflict realm.

## VII. Conclusions.

The Marine Corp's Tank community continues to refine how it operates in the mid to low intensity realm such as supporting counter insurgency operations. It must never lose focus on its ability to fight as that armored combined arms maneuver force that supports the Marine Division. Though many critics of heavy armor units proclaim that large scale conventional engagements are a thing of the past, the military as a whole must acknowledge that though it might be small the threat still exists. A review of three adversarial countries is all a military professional needs to look towards to observe some disturbing trends.

The country of North Korea has increased the number of its special warfare forces and battle tanks over the last two years as part of efforts to improve both conventional and asymmetrical military capabilities against South Korea, according to Seoul's latest defense white

paper.[35] North Korea has never been shy about its negative feelings toward the south and the

United States. It looks as if their Missile and Nuclear Testing aspirations are not the only

sources of interest when it comes to research and development.

> The white paper confirms the North has deployed a new battle tank, named "Pokpung-
> Ho," apparently based on the Soviet-built T-72. The North is also thought to have
> increased the number of its tanks from 2000 to about 4,100 for the past two years. In
> August of 2008, the North's Korean Central Television made public footage of the
> Pokpung-Ho (Storm), also dubbed the M-2002, has been presumed to have been rolled
> out from development since 2002. According to an analysis published by Seoul's
> Defense Agency for Technology and Quality, an affiliate of the Defense Acquisition
> Program Administration, the Pokpung-Ho is known to be armed with either a newly
> developed 125mm or 115mm main gun. The tank would also be mounted with a 14.5mm
> KPV anti-aircraft machine gun.[36]

Most individuals remember what happened in 1950 and the sight of North Korean Tanks moving

quickly south is not a sight anyone wants to see, but the prospect is not off any planning tables, it

seems.

Though the former Soviet Union does not make the front page of the newspaper as it did

during the Cold War, there still is a formidable threat from Russian ground force strength. When

the Russians invaded the small country of Georgia they demonstrated that they still have a very

strong offensive armor capability. After their observation of American offensive power with the

dominant M1A1 at the lead of the attack to drive Iraqi forces out of Kuwait they immediately

determined that they needed to mount a response in tank improvements.[37] The Russians

response to the observations of subpar performance of the T-72 and T-80 against the M1A1 led

research and development efforts to improvements applied to the Russian T-90. A larger main

gun was one of the biggest improvements to the T-90, they can be fitted with Explosive Reactive

Armor, and have been upgraded with laser rangefinders, an electromagnetic pulse generator to

combat magnetic mines, and they possess a new type of radar jamming system to scramble the guidance of incoming radar-guided anti-tank missiles.[38] All this effort to match up more

effectively with American tank technology and capability on a modern battlefield produces a

couple of very disturbing points: Russia's ability to mass produce equipment for its own use, or

its willingness to sell equipment to those who have not been overly friendly with the United

States. These points should encourage military leaders to revisit the efforts of Russian tank

development during World War II and consider how the mass production efforts of the T-34

provided the leverage for Russian armor units to defeat the technologically superior German

Panther along the Eastern front.

Then finally the country of China and its development of the Type 90 and 99 main battle

tanks, which are currently being upgraded in their arsenal. The whole world has witnessed the

massive growth of China's influence throughout the world in the last half of the 20th century and

the early portions of the 21st century. The country has always remained very guarded regarding

information about their military growth. The Communist government is adamant on controlling

what their populace understands about the outside world, and vice versa attempts to limit the

transit of information to the outside world. China has aggressively moved into virtually all areas

of the globe in the pursuit of access to natural resources to fuel their ever growing economy. As

they continue this effort to establish themselves in the world as a global power it is inevitable

that at some point in time they may have to conduct military actions against a competitor, one

such as the United States.

China is working hard on technology to influence the realm of space and cyber. They

have aggressive programs in anti-ship missile and radar development. Additionally, in the last

few years their research and development of an improved main battle tanks has received

considerable attention from Chinese tank researchers. The Russian HC Network published an article in September of 2010 noting, "that Chinese research and development of tanks in recent years has made great achievements and is expected to become the world's number one power in tank production".[39] Though the Chinese government has continued to procure the Russian-made T-90A, working to add further technological advancements to this platform, the Chinese have made a dedicated effort to improve their own Type 99 Main Battle Tank design.[40] The performance capability of these tank platforms is being significantly increased with an emphasis on speed, target identification, lethality of their main gun and enhanced survivability of armor protection. Aggressive improvements are being researched with the Type 99 to install a new fire control system that will increase thermal imaging ability for enhanced threat identification at greater ranges, along with an improved armor defense capability against kinetic energy munitions.[41] These systems, integrated into a Chinese tank design concept that has historically made main battle tanks with a small physical profile and limited turret, would make it a very survivable armor asset which could be employed with great effect in a defensive environment. The increased armor protection while maintain a small physical profile would make destroying it in a prepared defensive environment very difficult. The enhanced threat identification system that could be employed during day or night would only reinforce this defensive ability.

In pursuit of offensive power China has already begun mass production of improved 1,500 horsepower engine to propel their tanks at faster speeds, and successfully tested a new 140 millimeter tank main gun that could appear on newer models of their main battle tanks in the near future.[42] China has made huge strides in technology, space, cyber, and industrial production capability. All of these developments point toward a nation that understands it must be able to achieve decisive military strength in any arena. This recent trend to increase their ability to achieve a superior military capability on the ground in order to gain and maintain control of territory is an interesting movement. Maybe the era of major conventional conflict is not completely irrelevant, or a thing of the past, it is just lying dormant currently like a volcano until the times and circumstances are right for the next future conventional clash between competing interests.

Though the predominate threat might be from unconventional forces at the lower end of the conflict continuum scale, the Marine Corps should not fall into the belief that high intensity will never be a possibility. As stated during the introduction, Commandant General James Amos has challenged his Marines to ensure the force is prepared to carry out its mission as the United States force in readiness.[43] In order to effectively accomplish this task the Marine Corps must maintain a strong offensive capability that the Marine Tank Community brings to the fight. Fiscal constraints combined with downsizing the force in the next few years following 2011 present many significant challenges. A review will soon be released detailing how units across the Marine Corps will be affected. Due to the high cost associated with maintenance and operation the tank community has always been subject to a reduction in its force structure, or an outright deletion of the armor force from the Corp's ranks. Critics state that the requirement of maintaining heavy armored forces should be abandoned. If the Marine Corps wishes to operate throughout the entire spectrum of conflict, it is the belief of this author that the Corps must maintain an extremely powerful armor offensive capability. The Marine Corps will never, and should never, seek to just fill the roles of a second land army. However, if the Corps is serious about being a true middle weight force that can respond to a wide variety of conflict and be successful then it must maintain a wide array of combat capability that can be tailored to the mission and executed through the MAGTF concept in any theater of operation. The irregular and unconventional are definitely here to stay and Marine Tanks stand ready to provide that persistent presence that can deliver the heaviest volume of precision firepower on today's

modern day battlefield. Still, if history has taught a painful lesson to many past state powers, it

is that those who desire to achieve global influence have to possess a superior military capability

to effectively compete for resources from position of strength. The Marine Corps should refrain

from the thought that large scale conventional possibilities are completely extinct and ensure the

capability to compete with a conventional enemy is maintained. Marine Tanks have proven

themselves a decisive punch on past battlefields and continue to stand ready to deploy in any

integrated capacity, from platoon to battalion, to provide future MAGTFs the big punch to

America's middle weight fighting force.

---

[1] General Amos Speech at Shultz Lecture, February 8, 2011, http://www.marineclub.com/.

[2] General Amos Speech at Shultz Lecture, February 8, 2011, http://www.marineclub.com/.

[3] Otto Kreisher, Persian Gulf War: Marines' Minefield Assault. *The Quarterly Journal of Military History.* Summer 2002. http://www.jcsgroup.com/.

[4] Otto Kreisher, Persian Gulf War: Marines' Minefield Assault. *The Quarterly Journal of Military History.* Summer 2002. http://www.jcsgroup.com/.

[5] Brian Winters, Captain (USMC), After Action Report from Company B, 4th Tank Battalion.

[6] John Gordon IV and Bruce R. Pirnie. "Everybody Wanted Tanks: Heavy Forces in Operation Iraqi Freedom." *Joint Force Quarterly,* Issue 39, (December 2005). http://www.army.mil/.

[7] John Gordon IV and Bruce R. Pirnie. "Everybody Wanted Tanks: Heavy Forces in Operation Iraqi Freedom." *Joint Force Quarterly,* Issue 39, (December 2005). http://www.army.mil/.

[8] John Gordon IV and Bruce R. Pirnie. "Everybody Wanted Tanks: Heavy Forces in Operation Iraqi Freedom." *Joint Force Quarterly,* Issue 39, (December 2005). http://www.army.mil/.

[9] John F. Sattler (LtGen, USMC) and Daniel H. Wilson. "The Battle of Fallujah-Part II." *Marine Corps Gazette: Professional Journal of U.S. Marines,* July 2005, page 5.

[10] Kenneth Allard, "Somalia Operations: Lessons Learned". National Defense University Press Fort, Washington, D.C. January, 1995. Page 58.

[11] Dennis P. Mroczkowski, (Col. USMC, Ret.). *"Restoring Hope: In Somalia with the Unified Task Force, 1992-1993; U.S. Marine in Humanitarian Operations."* History Division, United States Marine Corps, Washington D.C. 2005., page 11.

[12] Dennis P. Mroczkowski, (Col. USMC, Ret.). *"Restoring Hope: In Somalia with the Unified Task Force, 1992-1993; U.S. Marine in Humanitarian Operations."* History Division, United States Marine Corps, Washington D.C. 2005., page 11.

[13] Marine Corps Combat Development Command. *Operation Restore Hope Collection and Lessons Learned Project Report.* Signed by C. C. Krulak, April 27, 1993. , page 2-C-20.

[14] Marine Corps Combat Development Command. *Operation Restore Hope Collection and Lessons Learned Project Report.* Signed by C. C. Krulak, April 27, 1993. , page 2-C-26.

[15] Dennis P. Mroczkowski, (Col. USMC, Ret.). *"Restoring Hope: In Somalia with the Unified Task Force, 1992-1993; U.S. Marine in Humanitarian Operations."* History Division, United States Marine Corps, Washington D.C. 2005., page 68.

[16] Marine Corps Combat Development Command. *Operation Restore Hope Collection and Lessons Learned Project Report.* Signed by C. C. Krulak, April 27, 1993. , page 2-C-2.

[17]Marine Corps Combat Development Command. *Operation Restore Hope Collection and Lessons Learned Project Report*. Signed by C. C. Krulak, April 27, 1993. , page 2-C-3.

[18]Mark Hickey, "The Marine Tank, the Proven Direct Fire Infantry Support Arm of Decision Within the MAGTF." Masters of Military Science, Marine Corps University Command and Staff College, 2009., page 9-10. Description of events from *After Action Report by Capt Campbell*, TF Mogadishu, 1993 pp354-355.

[19]Marine Corps Combat Development Command. *Operation Restore Hope Collection and Lessons Learned Project Report.* Signed by C. C. Krulak, April 27, 1993, page 2-C-2.

[11] Richard V. Mancini, "Placing the M1A1 Common Battle Tank Aboard Deploying Marine Expeditionary Units, Special Operations Capable." Masters Thesis, Marine Corps University Command and Staff College, 1995. Description of events from *After Action Report by Capt Campbell*, TF Mogadishu, 1993 pp354-355.

[21]Marine Corps Combat Development Command. *Operation Restore Hope Collection and Lessons Learned Project Report.* Signed by C. C. Krulak, April 27, 1993. , page 2-C-2.

[22]Marine Corps Combat Development Command. *Operation Restore Hope Collection and Lessons Learned Project Report.* Signed by C. C. Krulak, April 27, 1993. , page 2-C-2.

[23] James G. Zumwalt, "Let Somalia lesson factor in war strategy," *Stars and Stripes*, January 3, 2011, http://www.jgzumwalt.com/.

[24]James G. Zumwalt, "Let Somalia lesson factor in war strategy," *Stars and Stripes*, January 3, 2011, http://www.jgzumwalt.com/.

[25]James G. Zumwalt, "Let Somalia lesson factor in war strategy," *Stars and Stripes*, January 3, 2011, http://www.jgzumwalt.com/.

[26]James G. Zumwalt, "Let Somalia lesson factor in war strategy," *Stars and Stripes*, January 3, 2011, http://www.jgzumwalt.com/.

[27] James G. Zumwalt, "Let Somalia lesson factor in war strategy," *Stars and Stripes*, January 3, 2011, http://www.jgzumwalt.com/.

[28] John Gordon IV and Bruce R. Pirnie. "Everybody Wanted Tanks: Heavy Forces in Operation Iraqi Freedom." *Joint Force Quarterly*, Issue 39, (December 2005). http://www.army.mil/.

[29] Email from LtCol Barrick, Commanding Officer 1st Tank Battalion, 1st Marine Division (Rein).

[30] http://www.leatherneck.com/forums/showthread.php?t=29369.

[31] Email from LtCol Barrick, Commanding Officer 1st Tank Battalion, 1st Marine Division (Rein).

[32]Wesley Morgan, "Tanks to Afghanistan – Analysis." *NYTimes.com*, November 23, 2010, http://atwar.blogs.nytimes.com/.

[33] Defense Tech, Marines Want Tanks for Route Security, http://defenstech.org/.

[34] Wesley Morgan, "Tanks to Afghanistan – Analysis." *NYTimes.com*, November 23, 2010, http://atwar.blogs.nytimes.com/. Brig. Gen. U.S.A. H.R. McMaster has commanded the regiment in Tal Afar and has sence served as a key advisor to top generals in Iraq and Afghanistan.

[35] Jung Sung-Ki, Defense News (a Garnett Co.), http://www.defensenews.com/.

[36] Jung Sung-Ki, Defense News (a Garnett Co.), http://www.defensenews.com/.

[37]Future Weapon Technology, http://www.futurefirepower.com/.

[38] Future Weapon Technology, http://www.futurefirepower.com/.

[39]WAREYE, http://wareye.com/.

[40]WAREYE, http://wareye.com/.

[41]WAREYE, http://wareye.com/.

[42]WAREYE, http://wareye.com/.

[43]General Amos Speech at Shultz Lecture, February 8, 2011, http://www.marineclub.com/.

# Bibliography

Allard, Kenneth. "Somalia Operations: Lessons Learned". National Defense University Press Fort, Washington, D.C. January, 1995.

Barrick, Timothy E. (LtCol, USMC), "USMC Tank Vision Slides." Email posting dated January 28, 2011. timothy.barrick@usmc.mil.

Defense Tech, "Marines Want Tanks for Route Security." Posted December 17, 2010, http://defensetech.org/2010/12/17/marines-want-tanks-for-route-security/ (accessed February 27, 2011).

Future Weapon Technology, "The Newest Military Weapons System, Russian Tank Forces – 90 Technology and Chinese Type 99 Tank – Newest Armor of China." Posted on 25 August 2008, http://www.futurefirepower.com/category/tanks (accessed March 4, 2011).

Gordon, John IV and Bruce R. Pirnie. "Everybody Wanted Tanks: Heavy Forces in Operation Iraqi Freedom." *Joint Force Quarterly,* Issue 39, (December 2005). http://www.army.mil/professionalWriting/volumes/volume3/december_2005/12_05_3_pf .html (accessed February 26, 2011).

Hickey, Mark. "The Marine Tank, the Proven Direct Fire Infantry Support Arm of Decision Within the MAGTF." Masters of Military Science, Marine Corps University Command and Staff College, 2009.

Hoellwarth, John. "Making M1A1 more lethal." *Letherneck Magazine.com*, May 8, 2006. http://www.leatherneck.com/forums/showthread.php?t=29369 (accessed February 26, 2011).

Kreisher, Otto, Persian Gulf War: Marines' Minefield Assault.. *The Quarterly Journal of Military History.* Summer 2002. http://www.jcsgroup.com/military/navy_marine/1991persian.html (accessed February 26, 2011).

Mancini, Richard V. "Placing the M1A1 Common Battle Tank Aboard Deploying Marine Expeditionary Units, Special Operations Capable." Masters Thesis, Marine Corps University Command and Staff College, 1995.

Marine Corps Combat Development Command. *Operation Restore Hope Collection and Lessons Learned Project Report.* Signed by C. C. Krulak, April 27, 1993.

Morgan, Wesley. "Tanks to Afghanistan – Analysis." *NYTimes.com,* November 23,2010. http://atwar.blogs.nytimes.com/2010/11/23/tanks-to-afghanistan-analysis/ (accessed March 1, 2011).

Mroczkowski, Dennis P. (Col. USMC, Ret.). *"Restoring Hope: In Somalia with the Unified*

*Task Force, 1992-1993; U.S. Marine in Humanitarian Operations.* " History Division, United States Marine Corps, Washington D.C. 2005.

OFFICE OF COMMANDANT OF THE MARINE CORPS PREPARED REMARKS FOR THE GEORGE P. SHULTZ LECTURE GENERAL JAMES F. AMOS, COMMANDANT OF THE MARINE CORPS Tuesday, 8 February 2011; Marine Memorial Club, San Francisco, CA http://www.marineclub.com/documents/0211_GenAmosSpeechatShultzLecture110208.pdf (accessed February 17, 2011).

Sattler, John F. (LtGen, USMC) and Daniel H. Wilson. "The Battle of Fallujah-Part II." *Marine Corps Gazette: Professional Journal of U.S. Marines*, July 2005. http://www.mca-marines.org/gazette/operation-al-fajr

Sung-Ki, Jung, "N. Korea Boost Special Forces, Tanks: Report." Defense News a Gannett Company, published: December 30, 2010. http://www.defensenews.com/story.php?i=5342772 (accessed March 4, 2011).

WAREYE, "Russia Said the Main Battle Tank Production is Expected to Become the Number On Power (Figure)." Posted: Sep 25, 2010, http://wareye.com/russia-said-the-main-battle-tank-production-is-expected-to-become-the-number-one-power-figure (accessed March 4, 2011).

Winter, Brian M. (Capt, USMC), "After Action Report of Company B, 4th Tank Battalion, 4th Marine Division, Marine Forces Reserve during Operation Desert Storm", Yakima, Washington, February 26, 1991.

Zumwalt, James G. "Let Somalia lesson factor in war strategy." *Stars and Stripes*, Monday, January 3, 2011, http://www.jgzumwalt.com/index.php/articles/254-let-somalia-lesson-factor-in-war-strategy (accessed on 26 Feb 2011).

www.ingramcontent.com/pod-product-compliance
Lightning Source LLC
Chambersburg PA
CBHW062055090426

42740CB00016B/3141